TAYLOR SWIFT

in a
nutshell

*A Journey Through Music, Reinvention,
and Empowerment*

Felix Grayson

MINDSPARK
PUBLISHING

For the seekers of simplicity, the curious minds who crave the essentials without the fluff—this one's for you. Here's the story, in a nutshell.

"Brevity is the soul of wit."

— *William Shakespeare*

"Simplicity is the ultimate sophistication."

— *Leonardo da Vinci*

"Any fool can make something complicated. It takes a genius to make it simple."

— *Woody Guthrie*

IN A NUTSHELL'S PURPOSE

To provide quick, engaging overviews of pop culture, history, and trending topics, making it easy for readers to get the gist of any story.

IN A NUTSHELL'S MISSION

To deliver concise, entertaining content that educates and satisfies the curiosity of our readers and listeners in an ever-changing world of popular culture.

IN A NUTSHELL'S VISION

To be the go-to source for quick, digestible insights on the people, events, and trends shaping our world.

IN A NUTSHELL'S CORE VALUES

Simplicity: Making information clear, concise, and accessible.

Curiosity: Encouraging exploration and learning about diverse topics.

Entertainment: Providing facts in a fun and engaging way.

Timeliness: Keeping up with current events and trends.

CONTENTS

INTRODUCTION

Taylor Swift is more than just a pop star; she is a phenomenon—a dynamic force in music, culture, and business. Since bursting onto the country music scene as a teenager, she has continually reinvented herself, each time exploring new musical landscapes while remaining true to her identity as a storyteller. Her journey from a young, hopeful songwriter in Nashville to a global icon is not just a tale of chart-topping hits, but a story of resilience, creative evolution, and a deep connection with fans around the world.

This book delves into the multifaceted world of Taylor Swift, capturing her rise to stardom, her battles for artistic control, and her lasting impact on the music industry and beyond. Each chapter explores a different era of her career, examining the personal and professional milestones that have defined her path. From the heartache and joy of her early albums to the fearless experimentation of "Red" and "1989," and the raw introspection of "Folklore" and "Evermore," Swift's music has resonated with audiences of all ages.

But her legacy extends far beyond her melodies and lyrics. Swift has become a powerful business mogul, an advocate for artists' rights, and a voice for social issues, using her platform to promote change and empower others. Her decisions, from re-recording her masters to challenging the music industry's status quo, have sparked important conversations about ownership, fairness, and artistic freedom. Along the way, she has cultivated a devoted fan base—the Swifties—whose unwavering support and engagement have become an integral part of her story.

This book aims to offer a comprehensive look at the different facets of Taylor Swift's career, exploring how she has navigated fame, controversy, and success with poise and determination. It celebrates her artistry, her business acumen, and her courage to speak out on issues that matter. Whether you're a lifelong fan or simply curious about the woman behind the music, this journey through Swift's evolution will reveal how she continues to shape the world with her voice, her words, and her actions.

So, join us as we dive into the life and legacy of Taylor Swift: the musician, the businesswoman, the advocate, and the storyteller. This is not just the story of an artist—it's the story of a woman who has refused to be defined by others and, in doing so, has inspired millions to embrace their own narratives.

CHAPTER 1: EARLY LIFE AND BEGINNINGS

Childhood and Musical Roots

Taylor Swift was born on December 13, 1989, in Reading, Pennsylvania, and grew up in the nearby town of Wyomissing. Raised in a close-knit family, her parents, Scott and Andrea Swift, nurtured her creative spirit from a young age. Taylor's childhood was filled with a love for the arts; she was naturally drawn to storytelling, writing poems, and songs even before she could fully grasp the depth of her emotions. Her grandmother, a professional opera singer, was a significant influence, passing down a love for music and performance.

By the time Taylor was 9, her passion for music was undeniable. She became captivated by country music, often citing Shania Twain and Faith Hill as some of her earliest inspirations. Unlike many of her peers, who were listening to mainstream pop, Taylor found solace in the tales spun within country songs. Their raw honesty and vivid storytelling resonated with her and laid the foundation for her future songwriting style.

At just 10 years old, Taylor began performing

locally at fairs, festivals, and karaoke contests. Armed with a karaoke machine gifted by her parents, she sang covers of her favorite country songs, catching the attention of audiences with her confidence and talent. During this period, she also learned to play the guitar. A computer repairman taught her how to play three basic chords, a simple lesson that opened up a whole new world of songwriting possibilities for the young artist. By age 12, Taylor had already started writing her own songs, drawing from her personal experiences and emotions—a practice that would become her signature in the years to come.

Nashville Dreams

As Taylor's passion for music deepened, she and her family realized that staying in Pennsylvania would limit her potential. Nashville, Tennessee, the heart of country music, beckoned. At 11 years old, she visited Nashville with her mother, knocking on the doors of record labels along Music Row with demo CDs in hand, showcasing her cover songs. However, despite her evident talent, most executives were hesitant to take on such a young artist. While this could have been a discouraging setback, it only fueled her determination.

Taylor's parents recognized her commitment to pursuing music as a career. With their support, the Swift family made a life-changing decision: they would move to Nashville. This move was a testament to their belief in Taylor's dream, and they did everything they could to support her budding career. Her father even transferred to a Nashville office of the investment firm he worked for, while her mother focused on managing Taylor's career.

Settling in Hendersonville, a suburb of Nashville, Taylor continued to hone her craft. She began performing at local venues and worked with songwriters in Nashville to polish her songwriting skills. At 14, she became the youngest artist ever signed to Sony/ATV Tree publishing, the largest music publisher in the world. This achievement marked a significant step forward in her career, as it gave her access to professional songwriters who would help her further refine her lyrical storytelling.

The Big Break: Big Machine Records

Despite her contract with Sony/ATV, Taylor was restless. She wanted to be more than just a song-writer; she wanted to be a performer in her own right. However, the traditional path to stardom in the country music world was lined with obstacles, especially for a young girl who refused to conform to the industry's expectations. Her big break came when she caught the attention of Scott Borchetta, a record executive with a vision to start his own independent record label, Big Machine Records.

In 2005, Taylor signed with Big Machine Records, becoming the label's first artist. This was a groundbreaking moment for both Taylor and the label. Unlike the larger, more established record companies, Big Machine was willing to give Taylor the creative freedom she needed to shape her music and public persona. With the support of Borchetta and the resources of Big Machine, she began recording her debut album, "Taylor Swift."

During this time, Taylor maintained a rigorous work ethic. She was not only involved in writing the songs but also took an active role in the production process. Her debut album, released in 2006, was a reflection of her life as a teenager, filled with relatable narratives of love, heartache, and growing up. Her single "Tim McGraw," inspired by a high school relationship, became the album's lead track and a powerful introduction to Taylor's talent for blending personal experiences with universal themes.

First Songs and Recognition

"Tim McGraw" marked the beginning of Taylor Swift's career as a singer-songwriter in the country music scene. The song introduced her to a wide audience, showcasing her ability to craft stories that felt genuine and heartfelt. It didn't take long for the song to gain traction on country music charts, and the music video further amplified her presence, solidifying Taylor's image as a young country artist with crossover appeal.

The success of "Tim McGraw" was followed by other singles like "Teardrops on My Guitar," "Our Song," and "Picture to Burn." Each track resonated with listeners, particularly teenage girls who found Taylor's lyrics to be authentic reflections of their own experiences. "Teardrops on My Guitar," with its haunting melody and poignant lyrics, became a defining hit, proving that her music had the power to transcend beyond country radio into mainstream pop.

Her self-titled debut album was a commercial success, eventually earning multi-platinum status. Critics praised Taylor for her songwriting skills, noting that she had a maturity and emotional depth far beyond her years. This early recognition from both fans and critics set the stage for her rise to stardom. As she continued to tour, opening for major country acts, she built a loyal fan base known for their deep connection to her music and persona.

The accolades began to pour in, with Taylor receiving her first award nominations. Her career was on an upward trajectory, and the world was starting to take notice of this talented young artist. She had successfully transitioned from a small-town girl with big dreams to a rising star in the country music world, ready to leave an indelible mark on the music industry.

CHAPTER 2: RISE TO STARDOM

Debut Album: Taylor Swift

Released on October 24, 2006, Taylor Swift's self-titled debut album was a powerful intro-duction to her artistry and unique perspective as a teenager navigating the complexities of life and love. The album's themes were deeply personal, exploring subjects like first crushes, heartbreak, and the ups and downs of young relationships. While these themes were famil-iar in the realm of country music, what made Taylor's album stand out was her fresh, candid approach and the way she expressed raw emo-tions through her songwriting.

Musically, the album combined traditional coun-try elements with a pop-infused sound. Swift's lyrical storytelling, paired with catchy melodies, quickly gained her recognition in both country and pop circles. Songs like "Teardrops on My Guitar" and "Our Song" showcased her ability to write with sincerity and simplicity, resonat-ing with young audiences who felt that she was putting their own experiences into words.

"Teardrops on My Guitar" was one of the al-bum's standout tracks. It told the story of unrequited love and the pain of longing for someone who doesn't feel the same way. The song struck a chord with listeners, particularly teenage girls, and became an anthem for those navigating similar emotions. Its success on both country and pop charts demonstrated Taylor's crossover potential early in her career.

"Our Song," another hit from the album, became a defining moment for Taylor. Its lighthearted, playful tone and narrative about young love captivated fans and cemented her reputation as a skilled storyteller. The song's chart-topping performance on the Billboard Hot Country Songs made Swift the youngest person to single-handedly write and sing a number-one song on the chart. The album's commercial success, coupled with its relatable lyrics and catchy tunes, laid the groundwork for Swift's ascent in the music world.

Songwriting Prowess

While many country artists relied on professional songwriters to craft their hits, Taylor Swift set herself apart by writing or co-writing every song on her debut album. Her songwriting prowess was evident from the start, as she skillfully captured the raw, unfiltered emotions of teenage life. She wrote songs that were authentic and vulnerable, filled with vivid imagery and narrative details that gave listeners a glimpse into her inner world.

One of the key aspects of Swift's songwriting that resonated with fans was her knack for turning personal experiences into universal stories. Her songs often drew from her own life, making them feel genuine and relatable. Whether she was singing about the butterflies of a first crush or the heartbreak of unrequited love, her lyrics were imbued with a sense of honesty that made her stand out in a genre dominated by more formulaic approaches to songwriting.

In "Teardrops on My Guitar," for example, Swift sings about a real-life experience with a boy she liked in high school, transforming the situation into a poignant ballad that captured the essence of young, unfulfilled love. Similarly, in "Picture to Burn," she vented her frustrations about a breakup with a fiery, empowering tone that resonated with anyone who had ever felt the sting of rejection. This ability to infuse her music with genuine emotion and real-life scenarios helped her build a strong connection with her audience.

Taylor's commitment to writing her own material and her mastery of storytelling set her apart from other young artists of her time. She wasn't just singing songs; she was crafting narratives that spoke directly to the hearts of her listeners. Her songs became the soundtrack to many teenagers' lives, providing comfort, validation, and a sense of camaraderie through shared experiences.

Touring and Fan Base Building

In the wake of her debut album's success, Taylor Swift embarked on a grueling tour schedule, performing at various venues across the United States. She opened for established country acts like Rascal Flatts and George Strait, using every opportunity to showcase her talents to new audiences. These tours were instrumental in building her fan base, as she poured her heart and soul into each performance, winning over fans with her authenticity and charm.

From the very beginning, Taylor understood

the importance of connecting with her fans on a personal level. During her early tours, she made it a point to meet fans after shows, spending hours signing autographs and taking pictures. This dedication to her supporters created a loyal fan base that felt a deep personal connection to her. Swift treated her fans like friends, sharing personal stories, and responding to fan letters, which fostered a sense of community around her music.

Swift's live performances were not just concerts; they were storytelling experiences. She often introduced songs with anecdotes about their origins, giving the audience insight into the re-al-life events that inspired her lyrics. This story-telling element made her shows more engaging and allowed fans to feel a deeper connection to the music.

As she continued to tour, her fan base grew exponentially. Swift's dedication to her fans and her willingness to remain accessible set her apart in an industry where artists often main-tained a degree of separation from their audi-ences. This approach not only built a strong, devoted following but also laid the foundation for what would later become one of the most powerful fan communities in modern music: the "Swifties."

Awards and Recognition

Taylor Swift's debut album did more than just climb the charts; it garnered her critical acclaim and industry recognition, signaling that she was more than just a fleeting teenage sensation. In 2007, she received a nomination for the Academy of Country Music (ACM) Award for Top New Female Vocalist, and the following year, she won the award, a testament to her growing influence in the country music scene.

Her breakthrough moment came at the 2007 Country Music Association (CMA) Awards when she performed "Our Song." The performance captivated the audience and critics alike, showcasing her talents as both a vocalist and a performer. Later that year, she won the CMA Horizon Award, which recognized emerging talent in country music. This win was a significant milestone in her career, solidifying her place as a rising star in the genre.

In addition to her success at country music award shows, Taylor Swift also made inroads into mainstream pop culture. Her crossover appeal was evident when "Teardrops on My Guitar" entered the Billboard Hot 100, exposing her music to a broader audience beyond the country music world. Swift's ability to blend country roots with pop sensibilities marked her as an artist with the potential for longevity and mass appeal.

The recognition she received early on was not just for her vocal performance but also for her songwriting. In 2008, she was honored by the Nashville Songwriters Association International (NSAI) as Songwriter/Artist of the Year, making her the youngest person to receive this award. This acknowledgment from her peers in Nashville underscored her impact as a songwriter who could capture universal emotions through her music.

By the time her debut album cycle ended, Taylor Swift had established herself as a formidable force in the music industry. She had proven that she wasn't just another country singer; she was a storyteller, a performer, and a rising icon who had captured the hearts of millions. The foundation she built during this period set the stage for her meteoric rise to pop superstardom in the years that followed.

CHAPTER 3: FEARLESS AND THE CROSSOVER INTO POP

The Making of 'Fearless'

Following the success of her debut album, Taylor Swift set out to create her second studio album, "Fearless." Released on November 11, 2008, "Fearless" marked a turning point in Swift's career, showcasing her growth as a songwriter and artist. While still rooted in country music, the album saw her exploring a more polished sound that incorporated pop and rock elements, hinting at the musical evolution that would define her future work.

The creative process behind "Fearless" was a highly personal endeavor for Swift. She wrote or co-wrote every song on the album, a testament to her commitment to storytelling and her desire to maintain creative control over her music. Collaborating with established producers and songwriters like Nathan Chapman and Liz Rose, Taylor worked to refine her sound, blending her country roots with mainstream pop appeal. This fusion gave "Fearless" a broader, more universal reach while still preserving the authentic, narrative style that had endeared her to fans.

Lyrically, the album delved into themes of love, heartbreak, and self-discovery—subjects that resonated deeply with her audience. Songs like "Fifteen" drew from personal experiences, reflecting on the innocence and vulnerability of teenage relationships. Swift's storytelling prowess shone brightly in every track, with vivid imagery and relatable emotions that transported listeners into the highs and lows of adolescence.

Swift's meticulous attention to detail was evident in every aspect of "Fearless." From the songwriting to the production, she was deeply involved in the album's creation, striving to capture the raw emotions and experiences that had shaped her journey thus far. This dedication paid off, resulting in an album that felt both deeply personal and universally appealing, setting the stage for her crossover into mainstream pop music.

Chart-Topping Hits

"Fearless" produced some of Taylor Swift's most iconic hits, including "Love Story" and

"You Belong with Me," which played a crucial role in expanding her audience and solidifying her crossover appeal. These tracks showcased Swift's knack for crafting infectious melodies paired with lyrics that resonated with a wide range of listeners.

"Love Story," inspired by the tale of Romeo and Juliet, became one of Swift's signature songs. With its enchanting melody and romantic narrative, it captured the imagination of fans worldwide. The song's blend of country instrumentation and pop hooks made it a massive crossover success. Its accompanying music video, featuring a period-inspired love story, further amplified its appeal, creating a sense of timeless romance that resonated across different age groups. "Love Story" topped both country and pop charts, becoming one of the best-selling singles of all time and establishing Swift as a powerful force in the music industry.

"You Belong with Me" followed as another standout hit from the album. The song's relatable lyrics about unrequited love and longing for a high school crush struck a chord with listeners, particularly those who had experienced similar emotions. Swift's ability to articulate the complexities of teenage feelings in a way that felt both sincere and universal was key to the song's success. The accompanying music video, which depicted Swift as both the nerdy girl-next-door and the popular cheerleader, became iconic, earning heavy rotation on MTV and further boosting her visibility in the pop market.

The success of these singles expanded Swift's audience beyond the country music scene, drawing in fans from the pop and rock genres. "Fearless" spent weeks at the top of the Billboard charts, a clear indication of its widespread appeal. Taylor Swift had successfully bridged the gap between country and pop music, and her songs were now inescapable on both country radio and mainstream pop stations. This crossover was not just a shift in musical direction but a cultural moment that introduced Taylor Swift to a global audience.

The 'Fearless' Tour and Fan Connection

To promote "Fearless," Taylor Swift embarked on her first headlining tour, the "Fearless Tour," which ran from 2009 to 2010. This tour was a major milestone in Swift's career, showcasing her talents as a dynamic performer and solidifying her reputation as an artist who deeply valued her fans. The "Fearless Tour" featured elaborate stage setups, costume changes, and theatrical storytelling elements, creating an immersive experience that went beyond a typical concert.

Swift's dedication to connecting with her audience was a key highlight of the tour. She often took time during her performances to speak directly to fans, sharing personal stories and the inspirations behind her songs. This level of intimacy made her concerts feel like a conversation between friends, further strengthening the bond between Swift and her audience. One of the most memorable moments of each show was when Swift would venture into the crowd to hug fans and sing from different sections of the arena, making each performance feel unique and personal.

The tour was an enormous commercial success, selling out venues across North America, Europe, and Australia. Swift's ability to fill arenas at such a young age was a testament to her growing popularity and the powerful connection she had forged with her fan base. The "Fearless Tour" also featured a blend of her country hits and newer pop-leaning tracks, reflecting her musical evolution and preparing fans for the broader stylistic changes to come in her career.

During the tour, Swift continued her tradition of engaging with fans directly, spending hours after shows meeting with them, signing autographs, and taking photos. These interactions were crucial in building her loyal fan community, the "Swifties," who would go on to become one of the most dedicated and passionate fan bases in music history. Through the "Fearless Tour," Taylor Swift demonstrated that her success was not just about hit songs; it was about creating meaningful, lasting connections with her audience.

Awards and Accolades

"Fearless" catapulted Taylor Swift to new heights, earning her widespread critical acclaim and a slew of awards that solidified her place as a dominant force in the music industry. The album received praise for its blend of country and pop influences, as well as for Swift's songwriting, which was lauded for its honesty, maturity, and emotional depth.

One of the album's most significant achievements came at the 2010 Grammy Awards, where "Fearless" won Album of the Year. This victory made Swift the youngest artist ever to receive this honor at the time, a milestone that marked her transition from a country music star to a global pop icon. In addition to Album of the Year, she also took home three other Grammys, including Best Country Album, solidifying her impact on both the country and pop music scenes.

Beyond the Grammys, "Fearless" swept various award shows, winning accolades such as the Country Music Association (CMA) Awards for Album of the Year and the American Music Awards for Favorite Country Album. These wins underscored Swift's crossover success and highlighted the album's influence on the broader musical landscape.

The critical and commercial success of "Fearless" also garnered Taylor recognition from the Nashville Songwriters Association International (NSAI), which honored her as Songwriter/Artist of the Year for the second consecutive time. This acknowledgment from her peers in Nashville was particularly meaningful, as it affirmed her status as a songwriter whose storytelling transcended genres.

"Fearless" was more than just an album; it was a cultural phenomenon. It marked Taylor Swift's ascent from a talented young country artist to a mainstream pop sensation with a global reach. By the time the "Fearless" era concluded, Swift had established herself as a multifaceted artist with the power to shape the future of pop music. Her willingness to blend genres, her dedication to her craft, and her deep connection with her audience had positioned her not just as a country star but as a defining voice in contemporary music.

CHAPTER 4: REDEFINING HERSELF WITH 'RED' AND '1989'

Experimentation with 'Red'

By the time Taylor Swift began working on her fourth studio album, "Red," she was ready to explore new musical territories. Released on October 22, 2012, "Red" represented a period of experimentation for Swift, where she delved into various genres beyond her country roots. This album was a turning point, as it blended pop, rock, electronic, and even dubstep elements with her signature narrative style. It was clear that Swift was no longer content with being confined to the country music genre; she wanted to expand her horizons and challenge expectations.

"Red" was named after the intense emotions it conveyed—love, heartbreak, passion, and confusion—reflecting the tumultuous nature of Swift's personal experiences at the time. The album showcased her lyrical prowess, with each song serving as a vignette of complex feelings and relationships. Tracks like "All Too Well" revealed her storytelling at its most raw and vulnerable, while "Begin Again" offered a glimpse of hope amid heartbreak.

One of the most significant tracks on the album was "We Are Never Ever Getting Back Together." It was a bold departure from her previous work, featuring a more pop-oriented sound with infectious hooks and a conversational style. Produced by pop powerhouse Max Martin, the song captured the angst and frustration of a breakup with a catchy, sing-along chorus that resonated with listeners worldwide. Its success on the charts, reaching number one on the Billboard Hot 100, signaled Swift's growing influence in the pop music realm.

The album also featured songs like "I Knew You Were Trouble," which incorporated dubstep-inspired drops, a far cry from her earlier country ballads. This willingness to explore different genres while maintaining her confessional songwriting style set "Red" apart from anything she had done before. While some country purists were initially uncertain about the album's eclectic mix of sounds, fans embraced Swift's bold experimentation. "Red" marked a pivotal moment in her career, as it laid the groundwork for her full-fledged transition into pop music.

Embracing Full Pop: '1989'

Following the experimentation of "Red," Taylor Swift made a decisive move into the pop genre with her next album, "1989." Released on October 27, 2014, "1989" was a transformative project that saw Swift fully embrace her pop sensibilities, both sonically and aesthetically. Named after her birth year, the album was a homage to the synth-heavy pop of the 1980s, infused with Swift's modern touch.

The creative process behind "1989" was a departure from her previous work. Swift collaborated with producers and songwriters like Max Martin, Shellback, and Ryan Tedder to craft an album that was unapologetically pop. She swapped guitars for synthesizers and drum machines, opting for polished production and upbeat rhythms. The lyrics, while still personal, shifted away from the country storytelling tradition to embrace more abstract and metaphorical expressions of love, heartbreak, and self-discovery.

The album's lead single, "Shake It Off," was a celebration of individuality and resilience. It featured a vibrant horn section, an irresistible beat, and a playful music video that showcased Swift trying (and hilariously failing) to master various dance styles. "Shake It Off" became an anthem for self-empowerment, reaching number one on the Billboard Hot 100 and solidifying Swift's place in the pop world. The song's message—about brushing off criticism and embracing one's true self—resonated with a global audience, reflecting Swift's own journey of breaking free from expectations.

Another standout track from "1989" was "Blank Space," which addressed the media's portrayal of Swift's love life in a tongue-in-cheek manner. The song's clever lyrics and biting satire turned the narrative on its head, allowing Swift to reclaim control of her public image. With "1989," Swift made it clear that she was not just experimenting with pop; she was mastering it.

The album's success was monumental. It debuted at number one on the Billboard 200 chart, selling over a million copies in its first week, a feat unheard of in the era of digital music and declining album sales. "1989" marked the beginning of a new chapter for Swift, one where she redefined herself as a pop superstar with a global reach.

Visual Storytelling

As Swift's music evolved, so did her approach to visual storytelling. The music videos during the "Red" and "1989" eras played a crucial role in shaping her public persona and reinforcing the narratives of her songs. Swift's music videos became more elaborate, conceptual, and cinematic, serving as extensions of her artistry.

"Blank Space," in particular, was a game-changer. Directed by Joseph Kahn, the video portrayed Swift as a glamorous, yet unhinged, character in a lavish mansion, playfully exaggerating the media's depiction of her as a serial dater. The video featured dramatic scenes of jealousy, destruction, and revenge, embodying the tongue-in-cheek tone of the song. With its stunning visuals, intricate set design, and Swift's bold performance, "Blank Space" became an instant classic, accumulating millions of views and sparking conversations about her self-awareness and wit.

Similarly, "Bad Blood" took Swift's visual storytelling to new heights. Released as a single in 2015, the song's accompanying music video featured an ensemble cast of celebrities, including Selena Gomez, Gigi Hadid, and Zendaya, portraying a group of fierce female warriors. With its high-budget production, futuristic setting, and action-packed sequences, the video was a cinematic spectacle that drew attention to themes of betrayal, empowerment, and solidarity among women. It became a pop culture phenomenon, solidifying Swift's reputation as an artist who could create not just songs, but entire visual experiences.

These music videos were more than just promotional tools; they were narratives that allowed Swift to explore and control her image. By turning her music into visual art, she engaged fans on a deeper level, inviting them to interpret and analyze her work. This strategy not only kept her in the spotlight but also demonstrated her evolution as a multimedia artist who understood the power of storytelling across different platforms.

Global Stardom and Touring

With the success of "Red" and "1989," Taylor Swift's global stardom reached unprecedented levels, and her subsequent world tours became defining moments of her career. The "Red Tour," which spanned 2013 to 2014, was an extravagant spectacle that featured costume changes, intricate set designs, and dramatic performances. Swift's knack for blending theatricality with intimacy made her shows unique, leaving audiences captivated by both her storytelling and stage presence.

However, it was the "1989 World Tour" that truly showcased Swift's evolution into a pop icon. The tour, which kicked off in 2015, was a grand production, with elaborate stage setups, high-energy dance routines, and visual effects that turned arenas into immersive experiences. Swift's performances were meticulously crafted, featuring surprise guest appearances and mashups of her hits that kept the audience engaged from start to finish.

One of the standout elements of the "1989 World Tour" was Swift's interaction with her fans. She often took moments during the show to share personal stories, express gratitude, and acknowledge the fans' impact on her life and career. The tour also included a unique "B-stage" setup, where Swift would perform acoustic versions of her songs, creating an intimate atmosphere despite the massive stadium setting. These efforts reinforced her commitment to connecting with her audience, which had been a cornerstone of her career from the beginning.

The "1989 World Tour" was a commercial juggernaut, grossing over $250 million and attracting millions of fans across the globe. It not only showcased Swift's growth as a performer but also redefined what a pop concert could be. By combining storytelling, visual artistry, and fan engagement, Swift set a new standard for live performances in the pop music world. Her ability to transform large venues into spaces of collective celebration and personal connection made her concerts more than just shows—they were experiences.

By the end of the "1989" era, Taylor Swift had cemented herself as one of the most influential pop stars of her generation. Her willingness to embrace change, experiment with new sounds, and take control of her narrative allowed her to redefine herself in the public eye. With "Red" and "1989," Swift not only crossed over into pop but also reshaped the genre, leaving an indelible mark on the music industry.

CHAPTER 5: NAVIGATING CONTROVERSY AND REINVENTION

Public Feuds and Criticisms

As Taylor Swift's star rose higher, so did the scrutiny and criticism surrounding her personal life and public persona. In the midst of her journey to pop stardom, Swift found herself embroiled in several high-profile feuds that not only shaped public perception of her but also became pivotal moments in her career.

One of the most infamous episodes in Swift's career began at the 2009 MTV Video Music Awards (VMAs), when Kanye West interrupted her acceptance speech for Best Female Video. West's outburst, where he claimed that Beyoncé had the "best video of all time," sparked widespread media attention and became a defining moment in pop culture. While Swift initially responded with grace, the incident marked the beginning of a complicated relationship between the two artists that would resurface in later years.

The tension with Kanye West flared up again in 2016, when he released the song "Famous," containing a controversial lyric about Swift. The song reignited their feud and led to a very public spat involving Kanye, his wife Kim Kardashian, and Swift. Kim Kardashian released a series of Snapchat videos that appeared to show Swift approving the song's lyrics in a phone call with Kanye. Swift, however, maintained that she was not informed of the exact wording of the lyric that would be used, leading to a media storm and an onslaught of public backlash against her. The fallout was intense, with many accusing Swift of being manipulative and dishonest, resulting in the hashtag #TaylorSwiftIsOverParty trending on social media.

Another high-profile feud occurred with fellow pop star Katy Perry. Reports of tension between the two surfaced in 2013 over a dispute involving backup dancers, which was later confirmed through their music. Swift's song "Bad Blood," from her "1989" album, was widely speculated to be about the conflict with Perry, who responded with her own track, "Swish Swish." The feud was played out in the public eye, further contributing to the narrative of Swift as someone caught up in drama and rivalries.

These controversies cast Swift in a less favorable light, transforming her image from America's sweetheart into a lightning rod for public debate. The media began to scrutinize every aspect of her life, from her relationships to her actions, often framing her as a calculating, drama-driven figure. While some fans stood by her, others questioned her authenticity, creating a divide in public opinion that Swift would later address head-on in her music.

The 'Reputation' Era

In 2017, Taylor Swift unveiled her sixth studio album, "Reputation," a bold and dramatic response to the controversies and criticisms she had faced in the preceding years. With this album, Swift embraced a darker, edgier sound and image, stepping away from the light-hearted pop of "1989." The "Reputation" era was characterized by its exploration of themes like fame, media scrutiny, betrayal, and self-empowerment.

The album's lead single, "Look What You Made Me Do," was a stark departure from her previous work. The song's biting lyrics and haunting production revealed Swift's anger and frustration, targeting the media and those who had wronged her. In the song, she famously declares,

"The old Taylor can't come to the phone right now. Why? Oh, 'cause she's dead," signaling her transformation and rejection of her former image. The accompanying music video, filled with symbolism and references to her past, portrayed Swift as a woman reclaiming her narrative, unafraid to confront the controversies head-on.

"Reputation" as a whole was a defiant statement against the public scrutiny she had endured. Songs like "I Did Something Bad" and "This Is Why We Can't Have Nice Things" addressed the fallout from her feuds and the toxic media environment. The album's production, marked by heavy beats, synths, and a moody atmosphere, mirrored the intensity of its lyrical content. Swift worked closely with producers like Jack Antonoff and Max Martin to craft a sound that was bold, unapologetic, and reflective of her emotional state during this period.

Despite its darker tone, "Reputation" also explored themes of love and vulnerability, particularly in tracks like "Delicate" and "Call It What You Want." These songs offered glimpses of Swift's softer side, suggesting that while she was reclaiming her power, she was still capable of feeling love and pain deeply. The contrast between the album's fierce anthems and tender ballads underscored the complexity of Swift's character—she was not simply a victim or a villain but a multifaceted individual navigating the turbulence of fame.

Media Backlash and Reinvention

The release of "Reputation" was met with mixed reactions. Critics and the public were divided over Swift's new sound and image, with some praising her for her boldness and others questioning her motives. However, Swift was no longer seeking validation; "Reputation" was less about appeasing critics and more about reclaiming control of her narrative.

Swift used the album as a vehicle to confront the media's portrayal of her. In songs like "Blank Space" from the "1989" era, she had already shown her self-awareness of how the media caricatured her as a serial dater. But with "Reputation," she took it a step further, presenting herself as both a villain and a survivor, owning the persona that the media had painted. She refused to shy away from the controversies, instead using them as fuel for her reinvention.

In addition to her musical response, Swift became more private in her personal life during this period. After years of intense media coverage, she withdrew from the public eye, maintaining a low profile on social media and limiting her public appearances. This strategic retreat allowed her to regain a sense of control over her life and narrative. It also set the stage for a more deliberate and selective reemergence, one that emphasized her artistry and less on the tabloid fodder.

Swift's reinvention during the "Reputation" era was not just about embracing a darker image; it was about taking ownership of the story being told about her. By confronting her critics and controversies directly, she transformed herself from a target of media scrutiny into a powerful, self-possessed artist. This approach not only helped her navigate the backlash but also allowed her to redefine her identity on her own terms.

Rebuilding Trust with Fans

While "Reputation" was a declaration of self-em-powerment, Swift also recognized the need to reconnect with her fans, many of whom had followed her journey since her country music days. One of the key aspects of this era was her effort to rebuild trust with her audience through honesty, openness, and engagement.

Swift's "Reputation Stadium Tour," which spanned from 2018 to 2019, was a crucial part of this process. The tour was a spectacle, featuring elaborate stage designs, pyrotechnics, and an impressive setlist that spanned her entire career. Despite the grandeur, Swift made sure to create intimate moments during each show. She took time to speak directly to the audience, often addressing the themes of the "Reputation" album and the personal experiences that inspired it. This transparency resonated with fans, who appreciated her willingness to share her journey of growth and self-discovery.

The tour also included the return of Swift's famous "T-Party" sessions, where she invited fans backstage for private meet-and-greet sessions.

This gesture, reminiscent of her early career, reinforced her dedication to maintaining a personal connection with her supporters. By blending the spectacle of a stadium tour with moments of intimacy, Swift managed to bridge the gap that had formed between her and her fan base during the height of the controversies.

Moreover, Swift began to engage with fans on social media in a more deliberate manner. She interacted with their posts, commented on their stories, and even sent care packages to some of her most devoted supporters. These acts of kindness helped rebuild the sense of community that had always been a hallmark of her fan base.

Through her openness, humility, and focus on the music, Taylor Swift successfully navigated the fallout from her controversies and emerged stronger. The "Reputation" era was not just about defiance; it was about transformation, growth, and the reclamation of her narrative. By the time this chapter of her career ended, Swift had reestablished herself as an artist who was not defined by her critics but by her own resilience and authenticity.

CHAPTER 6: INDEPENDENT WOMAN – THE 'LOVER' AND 'FOLKLORE' ERAS

Breaking Free with 'Lover'

After the intense and dark energy of the "Reputation" era, Taylor Swift was ready for a new
chapter. In 2018, she made a crucial decision
that would shape the next phase of her career:
she left her longtime record label, Big Machine
Records, and signed with Republic Records and
Universal Music Group. This move gave her
ownership of her future master recordings—a
significant victory in an industry where artists
often lack control over their own work. Swift's
departure from Big Machine marked not just
a new contractual chapter but a personal and
artistic liberation that would be reflected in her
next album, "Lover."

Released on August 23, 2019, "Lover" was a
return to a lighter, more romantic sound. In contrast to the dark, defiant tones of "Reputation,"
"Lover" embraced themes of love, self-accep-
tance, and optimism. The album was a celebration of freedom—both creatively and personally.
Swift took on the role of executive producer,
asserting full control over the direction of her
music. The result was a colorful, genre-blending
album that explored various styles, from the

1980s-inspired synth-pop of "Cruel Summer" to the stripped-down balladry of "The Archer."

The album's title track, "Lover," was a heartfelt, old-fashioned love song, reminiscent of her earlier country ballads but with a more mature, nuanced perspective. Its simplicity and sincerity resonated with listeners, signaling Swift's return to her roots in storytelling, albeit with the wisdom of someone who had experienced and learned from life's complexities. Songs like "Paper Rings" and "London Boy" further showcased this playful, romantic side, filled with nostalgia and joy.

"Lover" also delved into themes of self-empowerment and social consciousness. Tracks like "The Man" critiqued gender inequality, with Swift examining how her life and career would be perceived if she were a man. "You Need to Calm Down" addressed societal issues, including homophobia, and demonstrated Swift's growing willingness to use her platform to advocate for causes she believed in.

With "Lover," Swift had not only broken free from the constraints of her previous record label but had also reclaimed her narrative. The album marked the beginning of a new era, one characterized by independence, creative exploration, and a renewed sense of self.

Creative Exploration: 'Folklore' and 'Evermore'

In 2020, as the world grappled with the COVID-19 pandemic and lockdowns, Taylor Swift surprised fans with a new direction in her music. On July 24, 2020, she released "Folklore," an album that marked a dramatic shift in style, venturing into indie-folk and alternative sounds. The surprise release of "Folklore" demonstrated Swift's ability to adapt and create in unexpected circumstances, showcasing her versatility as an artist and storyteller.

"Folklore" was a departure from the pop sensibilities of her previous work. It featured stripped-down arrangements, subdued melodies, and poetic lyrics that explored themes of nostalgia, loss, and introspection. Swift collaborated with producers and musicians like Aaron Dessner of The National and longtime collaborator Jack Antonoff to create a sound that was both minimalist and richly textured. The album felt like an intimate journal, filled with narratives and characters that blurred the line between personal reflection and fiction.

Tracks like "Cardigan" and "Exile," a haunting duet with Bon Iver, revealed a more somber, reflective side of Swift. In songs such as "The Last Great American Dynasty," she adopted a storytelling approach that ventured beyond her own experiences, recounting the history of the previous owners of her Rhode Island home. This shift in songwriting allowed her to explore different perspectives and experiment with narrative structures, illustrating her growth as a storyteller.

Just five months later, on December 11, 2020, Swift released "Evermore," a sister album to "Folklore." It continued the indie-folk direction, further exploring themes of introspection and storytelling. Songs like "Willow" and "Champagne Problems" echoed the wistful, ethereal quality of "Folklore," cementing this era as one of creative exploration and introspective artistry.

The release of "Folklore" and "Evermore" was a

testament to Swift's adaptability and her desire to experiment with her sound. These albums allowed her to step back from the highly polished pop productions of her previous work and instead focus on lyricism and mood. They also showcased her willingness to take risks and create art that resonated with the times, reflecting the stillness and uncertainty of the pandemic era.

Ownership and Re-Recording

A major chapter in Taylor Swift's journey as an independent artist was her battle for ownership of her master recordings. In 2019, it was revealed that Big Machine Records, the label she had left the previous year, had sold her entire back catalog to music executive Scooter Braun. This transaction meant that Swift did not own the rights to the master recordings of her first six albums, despite being the sole writer of most of her songs. The news sparked a public dispute between Swift and Braun, highlighting the broader issue of artists' rights within the music industry.

In response to this situation, Swift announced a

bold plan: she would re-record her first six albums to gain control over her music. This move
was both a personal statement and a business
strategy, aimed at devaluing the originals and
ensuring that she would own the new versions.
The re-recordings would allow her to license
her songs on her terms, shifting the power back
into her hands.

In 2021, she released "Fearless (Taylor's Version)," the first of her re-recorded albums. The
re-recording stayed true to the original while incorporating subtle changes and a more mature
vocal tone. The album also featured previously
unreleased tracks "from the vault," offering
fans new material alongside the familiar clas-
sics. "Fearless (Taylor's Version)" was met with
widespread acclaim and commercial success,
reaffirming Swift's influence in the industry and
her fans' support for her mission.

Swift's decision to re-record her catalog was
groundbreaking. It highlighted the importance
of artists owning their work and sparked conversations about industry practices related to
contracts and intellectual property. By taking
control of her narrative and music, Swift set an

example for other artists, showing that it was possible to fight for ownership and creative freedom in an industry often dominated by corporate interests.

Fan Engagement During the Pandemic

During the COVID-19 pandemic, when many artists faced challenges in connecting with their audiences, Taylor Swift found new ways to engage with her fans. While live performances and tours were off the table, Swift turned to social media and virtual interactions to maintain a close connection with her supporters.

The release of "Folklore" and "Evermore" during the pandemic was a direct result of this engagement. Swift communicated directly with fans through social media, sharing insights into her creative process and offering glimpses of her life in isolation. This transparency and openness resonated with listeners, many of whom found comfort in the reflective, quiet nature of her new music.

Swift also used platforms like Instagram Live to

interact with fans, often dropping hints about upcoming releases or explaining the stories behind her songs. Her efforts to keep fans involved and informed created a sense of community, even during a time of physical distancing. By staying connected with her audience, Swift reinforced the bond she had built over the years, reminding fans that they were part of her journey.

The "Folklore: The Long Pond Studio Sessions," a concert film released on Disney+, was another way Swift engaged with fans during the pandemic. The film offered an intimate look at the creation of "Folklore," featuring acoustic performances and discussions with her collaborators. It provided fans with a behind-the-scenes experience, deepening their connection to the music and to Swift as an artist.

Through these efforts, Swift demonstrated her commitment to her fans, even in uncertain times. Her ability to adapt to the changing circumstances of the pandemic and find new ways to share her art not only strengthened her fan base but also showcased her resilience and creativity as an independent woman in the music industry.

CHAPTER 7: THE BUSINESS MOGUL

The Power of Branding

From the outset of her career, Taylor Swift demonstrated a keen sense of branding, crafting a public image that resonated with her audience and evolved alongside her music. One of the keys to Swift's branding success has been her ability to create a persona that is authentic yet adaptable, allowing her to stay relevant in the ever-changing landscape of the music industry. Swift's brand identity—whether it was the country girl next door or the edgy pop icon—has always been meticulously curated, reflecting both her personal growth and artistic evolution.

A crucial component of Swift's branding strategy has been her use of merchandising. Throughout each album era, she created unique merchandise collections that echoed the themes and aesthetics of her music. During the "1989" era, for example, she embraced a retro-inspired, vibrant aesthetic, producing merchandise like T-shirts, polaroids, and accessories that captured the album's essence. With "Reputation," the branding took on a darker, edgier look, with snake motifs and gothic fonts. Similarly, for "Folklore" and

"Evermore," her merchandise featured earthy tones and whimsical designs, mirroring the albums' indie-folk sound.

Swift's approach to merchandise extends beyond traditional items. She has often created limited-edition products that align with specific moments in her career, such as exclusive vinyl pressings, autographed CDs, and unique holiday collections. By offering high-quality, thoughtfully designed products, Swift has fostered a sense of exclusivity and personal connection with her fans, turning her merchandise into coveted collectibles. This strategy not only generates additional revenue but also strengthens her relationship with her audience.

Collaboration has been another key aspect of her branding. Swift has partnered with various companies and designers to create products that reflect her artistic vision. For example, her collaboration with Keds in the early 2010s resulted in a line of sneakers that embodied her playful, feminine style. More recently, she partnered with Stella McCartney to launch a "Lover" fashion collection, merging music and high fashion in a way that appealed to her diverse fan base.

These collaborations allowed Swift to extend her brand beyond music, establishing her as a style icon and cultural influencer.

By creating a distinctive aesthetic for each album era and expanding her brand through collaborations and merchandise, Taylor Swift has cultivated a multifaceted identity that resonates with fans and consumers alike. This branding power has been instrumental in her success as both an artist and a business mogul.

Re-Recording Her Masters

In 2019, Taylor Swift made headlines with her announcement that she would re-record her first six albums. This decision came after her former record label, Big Machine Records, was acquired by music executive Scooter Braun, transferring ownership of the masters of her early catalog to Braun. Swift publicly expressed her dismay at the sale, revealing that she had been trying to purchase her masters for years, only to be met with restrictive conditions.

Swift's decision to re-record her albums was a bold and unprecedented move in the music industry. By creating new versions of her songs, she aimed to take back control of her work and offer fans an alternative to the originals owned by Braun's company. The re-recordings, branded as "Taylor's Version," were not just about reclaiming her rights; they were a statement against the industry's practice of withholding master ownership from artists.

The release of "Fearless (Taylor's Version)" in 2021 marked the beginning of this re-recording project. The album was meticulously crafted to remain faithful to the original while incorporating slight production nuances and a matured vocal performance. In addition to re-recording the original tracks, Swift included unreleased "From the Vault" songs, offering fans a new listening experience. This approach not only encouraged fans to embrace the new versions but also added value to the re-recordings, making them more than just replicas of the past.

Swift's fight for ownership sparked a broader conversation about artists' rights within the music industry. Historically, record labels have often held the rights to master recordings, leaving artists with little control over how their music is used or distributed. Swift's decision to re-record her catalog challenged this norm, empowering other musicians to advocate for their rights and negotiate better contracts. Her actions underscored the importance of artists owning their creative work, setting a precedent for future generations in the industry.

The success of "Taylor's Version" releases demonstrated Swift's influence and the loyalty of her fan base. Fans rallied behind her, purchasing and streaming the new versions, further diminishing the commercial value of the original masters. Swift's campaign for ownership became a powerful example of how artists can reclaim their narrative and assert their agency within a system that often prioritizes profit over creativity.

Taylor Swift as an Advocate

In addition to advocating for her own rights, Taylor Swift has used her platform to speak out on behalf of artists and creators within the music industry. One of her most notable actions was her open letter to Apple Music in 2015. At the time, Apple planned to offer a three-month free trial of its new streaming service without compensating artists during that period. In a candid and impassioned letter, Swift criticized the policy, arguing that it was unfair to expect musicians to work for free, especially those who were just starting their careers.

Swift's letter quickly gained public support, prompting Apple to change its policy and agree to pay artists during the free trial period. This victory was a testament to Swift's influence and her commitment to fighting for fair compensation for artists. It also highlighted the power of established musicians using their platform to advocate for systemic change within the industry.

Swift continued her advocacy in 2018 when she signed with Republic Records and Universal Music Group. As part of her new deal, she negotiated that any sale of Universal's Spotify shares would result in a distribution of profits to all of its artists, not just those at the top. This move demonstrated her dedication to improving conditions for her peers and setting a new standard for artist-label agreements.

Through these actions, Swift has positioned herself as a champion for artist rights. Her willingness to speak out, negotiate fair terms, and challenge industry practices has not only benefitted her but also set a precedent for other musicians seeking to take control of their careers. By advocating for transparency, fair compensation, and creative ownership, Swift has become a powerful voice for change within the music world.

Diversification Beyond Music

While music remains her primary focus, Taylor Swift has diversified her career into various fields, establishing herself as a multifaceted businesswoman. One of her early ventures outside of music was in fashion. Swift's style evolution over the years has turned her into a fashion icon, leading to collaborations with brands like Keds and Stella McCartney. Her influence on fashion trends, from the country-inspired boots and dresses of her early years to the high-fashion looks of her "1989" and "Reputation" eras, has cemented her place in the industry.

Swift has also made forays into acting and film. She appeared in movies such as "Valentine's Day" (2010) and "The Giver" (2014), showcasing her versatility as an artist. In 2019, she starred in the movie adaptation of the musical "Cats." While the film received mixed reviews, Swift's involvement highlighted her interest in exploring different forms of creative expression. She also contributed to film soundtracks, such as writing and performing the song "Beautiful Ghosts" for "Cats," which garnered critical acclaim.

Moreover, Swift has been actively involved in social causes, using her platform to advocate for issues she believes in. She has spoken out on topics ranging from LGBTQ+ rights to gender equality and voter participation. In 2019, she publicly endorsed political candidates for the first time, urging her fans to vote and engage in the democratic process. Swift's activism reflects her understanding of the influence she wields and her desire to use it for positive change.

Her involvement in these ventures demonstrates

Swift's business acumen and her ability to expand her brand beyond the music industry. By diversifying her career, Swift has not only built a successful business empire but also solidified her legacy as a dynamic, multifaceted artist and entrepreneur.

Through her branding, re-recording campaign, advocacy for artists, and ventures outside of music, Taylor Swift has proven herself to be more than just a pop star—she is a savvy business mogul who continually redefines what it means to be a modern artist in an ever-evolving industry.

CHAPTER 8: LEGACY AND IMPACT

Influence on Music and Pop Culture

Taylor Swift's impact on modern music and pop culture is both profound and multifaceted. Since the release of her debut album, Swift has continually pushed the boundaries of genre and redefined what it means to be a female artist in the music industry. Her influence can be seen in the way she has shaped modern songwriting, embraced genre crossover, and inspired a new generation of artists.

One of Swift's most significant contributions to music is her approach to songwriting. From the beginning of her career, she has been known for her deeply personal lyrics, using her own life experiences as the foundation for her songs. This autobiographical style has resonated with fans, offering them a glimpse into her emotions and experiences. Swift's storytelling prowess, marked by vivid imagery, emotional honesty, and narrative detail, has set a high standard for lyricism in contemporary music. Many artists who followed in her footsteps have adopted a similar confessional style, making personal storytelling a defining characteristic of modern pop.

Swift's ability to blend genres has also had a lasting impact on the music industry. Starting as a country artist, she gradually transitioned into pop, incorporating elements of rock, electronic, and indie-folk into her music along the way. Albums like "Red" and "1989" demonstrated how an artist could successfully straddle different genres without losing their unique voice. This genre fluidity has encouraged other musicians to experiment with their sound, breaking down the rigid barriers between musical categories. Today, the music industry is more open to genre crossover, with artists frequently drawing from diverse influences to create their own distinct soundscapes.

Furthermore, Swift has played a crucial role in amplifying the voices of women in the music industry. By writing and co-producing her own songs, she has asserted her creative authority and challenged the male-dominated structures of the industry. Swift's visibility and success have empowered other female artists to take charge of their careers, pursue songwriting, and demand greater control over their work. Her advocacy for artist rights, particularly her fight to own her master recordings, has underscored the importance of female musicians asserting their agency in an industry that often prioritizes profit over artistry.

The Swifties: A Powerful Fandom

A key part of Taylor Swift's legacy is the dedicated and passionate fan base she has built over the years. Known as "Swifties," her fans are more than just listeners; they are an active community that has played a vital role in promoting her music and shaping her career. From supporting her during controversies to celebrating her achievements, Swifties have become a powerful force in the music industry.

Swift has cultivated this fandom through her genuine connection with fans. From the early days of hosting meet-and-greets after her shows to interacting with fans on social media, she has always made an effort to bridge the gap between artist and audience. She often leaves clues about her upcoming projects in her social media posts, music videos, and lyrics, encouraging fans to piece together information in what they refer to as "Easter egg hunts." This sense of involvement creates an interactive experience that keeps fans engaged and invested in her work.

Swifties have also proven to be a driving force in promoting her music. They organize streaming parties to boost her song's chart performance, create fan art, and actively participate in online discussions, keeping Swift's name and music in the spotlight. Their dedication extends to supporting Swift's re-recording campaign, where they have embraced "Taylor's Version" releases as a way of standing in solidarity with her fight for artistic ownership.

The sense of community within the Swiftie fandom has been a crucial element of Swift's continued success. By fostering an environment where fans feel seen, heard, and valued, she has built a loyal following that transcends generational and geographical boundaries. This powerful fandom not only amplifies her music but also provides a network of support that has helped her navigate the highs and lows of her public life.

Activism and Social Influence

In addition to her musical legacy, Taylor Swift has made her mark as a social advocate. Over the years, she has used her platform to speak out on various issues, including feminism, LGBTQ+ rights, and political activism. Her outspokenness has not only influenced public discourse but has also shaped her public image as an artist who is unafraid to address important topics.

Swift's advocacy for women's rights has been a consistent theme throughout her career. She has often spoken out about the challenges women face in the music industry, from unequal pay to the objectification and scrutiny of female artists. In songs like "The Man," she confronts the double standards that women encounter, imagining how her life and career would be perceived if she were a man. Swift's willingness to tackle these issues has inspired conversations about gender inequality and has encouraged her fans, particularly young women, to stand up for their own rights.

Her support for the LGBTQ+ community became more visible during the "Lover" era. In her song "You Need to Calm Down," Swift calls out homophobia and advocates for equality, aligning herself with the LGBTQ+ movement. She also publicly voiced her support for the Equality Act, urging her fans to sign a petition in favor of legal protections for LGBTQ+ individuals. This advocacy marked a shift in Swift's public persona, from a traditionally apolitical figure to one who openly champions social causes.

Swift's involvement in political activism became even more pronounced in the lead-up to the 2018 midterm elections. For the first time, she publicly endorsed political candidates, taking a stance on issues such as gender discrimination, LGBTQ+ rights, and racial inequality. Her post, which encouraged fans to register to vote, had a measurable impact, with voter registration spiking in the days following her endorsement. By leveraging her platform in this way, Swift demonstrated the power of celebrity influence in shaping public engagement with social and political issues.

Through her activism, Swift has solidified her position as more than just a musician; she is a cultural figure who uses her voice to advocate for change. Her actions have further shaped her public image as an artist who is not only dedicated to her craft but also committed to making a positive impact on society.

What's Next for Taylor Swift

As Taylor Swift continues to evolve as an artist and public figure, speculation abounds about the future directions she might pursue. Given her history of reinvention and exploration, it is likely that Swift will continue to surprise and challenge expectations with her next creative endeavors.

One possible direction is further exploration into film and storytelling. Swift has shown a keen interest in visual storytelling, as seen in her music videos and her work on "All Too Well: The Short Film," which she wrote, directed, and starred in. This foray into filmmaking suggests that she may continue to explore opportunities in the world of cinema, perhaps expanding her role as a director, screenwriter, or even actor in larger projects. With her talent for narrative and her ability to connect with audiences emotionally, it would not be surprising to see Swift make a name for herself in the film industry.

Musically, Swift may continue to experiment with different genres. The indie-folk sound of "Folklore" and "Evermore" showcased her versatility, proving that she can excel in various musical styles. Fans and critics alike are eager to see where she takes her sound next, whether it be a return to pop, a deep dive into rock or electronic music, or another unexpected genre. Given her track record, Swift is likely to approach her future projects with the same creativity and innovation that has defined her career thus far.

In addition, Swift's commitment to advocacy and ownership suggests that she may further involve herself in the business side of the music industry. As she continues to re-record her earlier albums, she is poised to become a case study in artistic autonomy and the importance of artists' rights. Swift may use her experiences to educate and support other musicians, potentially becoming a mentor or advocate within the industry. Her influence could lead to meaningful changes in how record labels and artists negotiate ownership and rights.

Whatever path she chooses, one thing is certain: Taylor Swift's legacy will continue to grow. She has already left an indelible mark on music, pop culture, and social discourse, and her ongoing journey promises to add new dimensions to her impact. Swift's ability to adapt, reinvent, and engage with her audience ensures that her influence will endure for years to come.

CONCLUSION

Taylor Swift's journey from a young country music prodigy to a global pop icon has been nothing short of extraordinary. Over the past decade and a half, she has redefined what it means to be a modern artist—one who is not only musically gifted but also business-savvy, socially conscious, and unafraid of reinvention. Her story is one of resilience, creativity, and the relentless pursuit of authenticity in an industry that often demands conformity.

From her early days in Nashville, strumming a guitar and writing about teenage love, to her exploration of diverse musical styles, Swift has remained true to her core: a storyteller. Her lyrics, marked by raw honesty and vivid imagery, have connected with millions, turning personal experiences into universal anthems. This commitment to honest, introspective songwriting has set her apart, inspiring a new generation of artists and redefining the art of modern pop.

Swift's influence extends far beyond her music.

Her business acumen, as seen in her battle for ownership of her master recordings and her strategic branding, has challenged industry norms and empowered other musicians to assert their rights. Through her advocacy for artist compensation, gender equality, and social justice, she has used her platform to effect change, demonstrating that artists can—and should— play an active role in shaping the cultural and social landscape.

Her devoted fan base, the Swifties, is a testament to the power of community in an era dominated by digital interactions. By fostering a personal connection with her audience and maintaining an ongoing dialogue with them, Swift has built a support system that has propelled her through the highs and lows of her career. This unique relationship with her fans has not only contributed to her commercial success but has also made her a beloved figure in pop culture.

As Taylor Swift continues to evolve, the future promises new artistic ventures and further influence in both music and beyond. Whether through genre exploration, storytelling in film, or continued advocacy for artists' rights, Swift's legacy will continue to grow and inspire. She stands as a shining example of how an artist can take control of their narrative, adapt to challenges, and remain true to their creative vision.

In every era, Swift has shown that success in music is not just about chart-topping hits, but about authenticity, perseverance, and the courage to reinvent oneself. As she moves forward, her journey serves as a reminder that the impact of a true artist goes far beyond the music—it lies in the stories told, the lives touched, and the lasting change inspired.

WANT MORE IN A NUTSHELL?

Curious for more quick, engaging reads that make complex stories simple?

The *In a Nutshell* series offers concise, entertaining overviews of pop culture, history, and trending topics—perfect for readers who love to learn, laugh, and stay informed.

Explore the full *In a Nutshell* collection and discover other books and audiobooks by **Felix Grayson**, published by **MindSpark Publishing**.

Visit **FelixGrayson.com** to see what's new,

what's trending, and what's next.

Big ideas don't need big books.

Sometimes, the best stories fit perfectly—in a nutshell.

ACKNOWLEDGEMENT

I would like to extend my deepest gratitude to Taylor Swift, whose incredible journey and artistry inspired this book. Her dedication to storytelling, advocacy, and creativity has left an indelible mark on music and culture.

A heartfelt thank you goes out to the Swifties—the dedicated fan base that has supported and uplifted Taylor's work throughout the years. Your passion and commitment are a testament to the powerful connection that music can create.

Finally, to all those who continue to explore, analyze, and celebrate the art of music: your curiosity and love for storytelling make projects like this possible. Here's to the ongoing legacy of artists who dare to dream, inspire, and change the world with their voice.

ABOUT THE AUTHOR

 Felix Grayson has always been fascinated by the stories that shape our culture — from defining historical events to the moments in pop culture that captivate millions. With a lifelong passion for storytelling and discovery, Felix brings clarity and insight to complex topics, making them accessible, engaging, and fun to explore.

As the creator of the *In a Nutshell* series, Felix combines thoughtful research with concise storytelling to deliver quick yet meaningful over-views of the people, events, and trends shaping our world. His mission is simple: to make learning enjoyable for everyone, no matter how busy life gets.

When he's not diving into the latest cultural phenomenon or uncovering forgotten chapters of history, Felix enjoys connecting with readers, sharing ideas, and exploring new stories—one nutshell at a time.